ELECTRONIC WIZARDS

ELECTRONIC WIZARDS
CROWS, ZAPPERS & WEASELS

René J Francillon, Peter B Lewis & Jim Dunn

Acknowledgements

Additional photography by Boeing, Ken Buchanan, Tony Holmes, Robert S Hopkins III, Robert E Kling, Lockheed, Rick Morgan, Masanori Ogawa, Carl E Porter, Mick Roth, and the United States Air Force.

Published in 1991 by Osprey Publishing Limited
59 Grosvenor Street, London W1X 9DA

British Library Cataloguing in Publication Data
Francillon, René J. (René Jacquet), 1937 —
    Electronic wizards: Crows, Zappers and Weasels.
    1. Electronic warfare. Aircarft
    I. Title   II. Lewis, Peter B.   III. Dunn, Jim
    623.746

ISBN 1855321122

Editor Tony Holmes
Page Design Paul Kime
Printed in Hong Kong

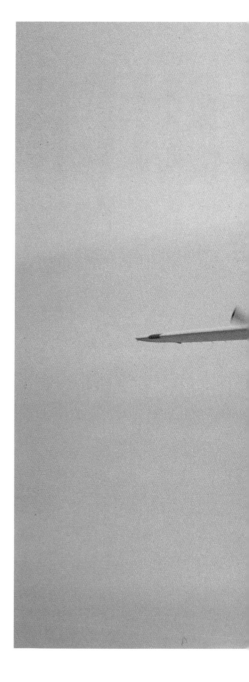

Front cover Flaps and slats deployed, a glossy E-3C sentry from the 965th Airborne Warning and Control Squadron glides in on approach to Nellis AFB during a *Red Flag* exercise in 1990. Deployed to the Persian Gulf within months of this photo being taken, the 965th flew hundreds of sorties in support of *Operation Desert Shield (Peter B Lewis)*

Back cover Looking good for a safe recovery at RAF Mildenhall after a surveillance sortie over the North Sea, RC-135W, 62-4139, returns home. Although flown by aircrew from the 38th Strategic Reconnaissance Squadron (SRS), the mission electronics specialists come from the 343rd SRS *(Air Portraits)*

Title Page Carrying AIM-9 Sidewinder air-to-air missiles for self-defence, a Wild Weasel F-4G from the 562nd TFTS, 37th TFW, is refuelled by a KC-10A during a training sortie on 8 August 1986

For a catalogue of all books published by Osprey Aerospace
please write to:

**The Marketing Manager, Consumer Catalogue Department
Osprey Publishing Ltd, 59 Grosvenor Street, London, W1X 9DA**

Above A Lockheed EC-130H of the 41st Electronic Combat Squadron, Tactical Air Command, landing at Nellis AFB, Nevada, at the end of a Green Flag sortie on 11 April 1988

Introduction

For US forces, the era of electronic warfare began in 1942–43 with three significant operations undertaken over widely separated areas. On 31 October 1942, a member of the Navy's first countermeasures team (designated Cast Mike 1 in the phonetic alphabet of the time) used, without success, an intercept receiver installed in a B-17E of the 11th Bomb Group, USAAF, to search for Japanese radar signals in the Solomon Islands. Between 6 and 15 March 1943, 'ferret' specialists from the Army Air Forces flew three sorties in a specially modified B-24D to obtain detailed Japanese radar coverage in and around Kiska before US forces undertook the reconquest of this Aleutian island. Finally, during the night of 9/10 July 1943, four B-17Fs of the 16th Reconnaissance Squadron flew the first radar jamming sorties during the invasion of Sicily.

In the later phases of World War 2, the use of various forms of electronic countermeasures – notably chaff or 'window' to confuse enemy radar during heavy bomber raids; deceptive jamming to create a fake fleet during Operation Overlord; and the active jamming of AAA fire control radar during B-29 operations against Japan, became an accepted component of major military operations. However, it was during the Cold War that COMINT, ELINT, SIGINT, TELINT (communications, electronic, signal, and telemetry intelligence) gained their prominent status. Eventually, the threat of surface-to-air missiles (SAMs) during the South-east Asian War, added a new dimension to electronic warfare with the development of specialized tactics and equipment for defence suppression (Navy aircraft destroyed their first SAM sites during Iron Hand strikes on 27 July 1965, and the first successful Wild Weasel mission was flown by the Air Force on 22 December 1965).

Although far from being exhaustive, this collection of photographs illustrates most of the principal types of electronic warfare aircraft operated by US forces during the past quarter of a century for defence supression, intelligence gathering, C^3 (command, control and communications), electronic warfare, electronic training (aggressor operations), and RDT&E (research, development, test & evaluation).

René Francillon, Peter B Lewis, and Jim Dunn
Vallejo, California, January 1990

Right Jammed in amongst other members of CVW-14, this EA-6B of VAQ-139 'Cougars' started life as an Improved Capability (ICAP) 1 machine, before being returned to Grumman in the mid-1980s for updating to ICAP 1 MOD standards. Looking extremely weather-beaten, even by US Navy standards, this VAQ-139 machine, on board USS *Constellation* (CV-64), had just returned from 79 consecutive days on station in the Indian Ocean and North Arabian Sea supporting Persian Gulf convoy operations. An integral part of Battle Group Delta, 'Connie's' Westpac '87 cruise had seen the carrier heavily involved in escort duties up and down the Persian Gulf, the 'Cougars' flying their fair share of convoy patrols during this tense period *(Tony Holmes)*

Contents

Defence Suppression

Left Based at McConnell AFB, Kansas, the 561st TFS, 23rd TFW, took 12 F-105Gs to Korat Royal Thai Air Force Base (RTAFB), Thailand, in April 1972 as part of the Constant Guard II deployment of USAF units which was undertaken in answer to the North Vietnamese invasion of South Vietnam in the spring of 1972

Overleaf The last unit to fly the F-105G was the 128th TFS, Georgia ANG, at Dobbins AFB. Aircraft 63-8363 was photographed at this base late in the afternoon of 18 October 1982

Opposite Bearing the 'GA' tail code of the 35th TFW, this F-105G of the 563rd TFS was photographed on the ramp at George AFB, California, on 15 March 1974

Top A Republic EF-105F (63-8284) at McClellan AFB on 2 June 1971. Small antennae for the AN/APR-25 system, one of the features distinguishing Wild Weasel EF-105Fs from combat trainer F-105Fs, are barely visible behind the radome. The first five EF-105Fs were deployed to Korat RTAFB in May 1966 and EF-105Fs made their first radar kill on 7 June 1966

Above Republic F-105G (63-8306) of the 563rd TFS, 35th TFW, at Mather AFB on 5 April 1975

Left Part of the 37th TFW at George AFB, this aircraft is assigned to the 562nd TFTS, the USAF's Wild Weasel training squadron. Captured recovering at Nellis on 21 August 1987, this Wild Weasel (69-0256) has an AGM-88 HARM (High-speed Anti-Radiation Missile) round mounted to its inner portwing pylon

Below The Wild Weasel's main weapon is the AGM-88 HARM seen here mounted on a F-4G at George AFB

Left This F-4G (69-7287) belongs to the 561st TFS, 37th TFW, at George AFB, and was seen on 12 August 1986

Above A 37th TFW pilot at George AFB on 12 August 1986 takes care of the necessary paperwork before a training flight. Even a Wild Weasel cannot weasel his way out of paperwork!

Previous pages An F-4G of the 23rd TFS, 52nd TFW, from Spangdahlem AB, Germany, at Chièvres, Belgium, on 25 June 1989

Above A pair of aces; an F-16C and an F-4G from the 52nd TFW, USAFE, return from 'hunting' simulated defences on the Nellis range during Green Flag 1988

Left To complement its small force of Wild Weasels, the USAF is increasingly pairing F-4G 'hunters' with F-16C 'killers' such as this HARM-carrying Fighting Falcon of the 23rd TFS photographed at Chièvres, Belgium, on 25 June 1989

During the war in South-east Asia, 19 A-6As were modified as A-6B defence suppression aircraft. Five were lost during the war and the remaining 14, including this ex-VA-34 aircraft photographed at Davis-Monthan AFB on 13 March 1976, were brought up to A-6E standard between December 1975 and December 1979

Above When operating in the defence suppression role, a singularly risky operation for an aircraft as valuable as the Prowler, EA-6Bs carry AGM-88 HARM missiles. Along with other squadrons of CVW-15, the 'Garudas' of VAQ-134 worked up at NAS Fallon in June 1989 before deploying aboard the USS *Carl Vinson* (CVN-70)

Right Not often seen toting anything other than ALQ-99 jamming pods beneath its wings, this 'Garuda bird' of VAQ-134 has just returned from a training sortie over the 'electric' ranges at NAS Fallon on 21 June 1989

Unlike the Air Force, the US Navy no longer has specialized defence
suppression aircraft. Instead the task is performed by A-7Es, F/A-18s and
EA-6Bs armed with anti-radiation missiles. This particular Corsair, BuNo
160613, belongs to the 'Clansmen' of VA-46 who regularly cruise the Atlantic
with CVW-3 aboard the USS *John F Kennedy* (CV-67)

An F/A-18A of VFA-195 'Dambusters', one of three Hornet squadrons homeported at NAS Atsugi, Japan, for deployment aboard the USS *Midway* (CV-41), seen here at NAS Fallon, Nevada, in October 1986. The aircraft is carrying an AGM-88 HARM missile

Intelligence Gathering

Always impressive, the SR-71 is not over attractive on the ground. In the air, however, it is a truly beautiful aircraft, especially when seen powering in towards a KC-135Q tanker. Aircraft 64-17976 is pulling away from the tanker after refuelling for the second time during the course of a training sortie lasting slightly over three hours on 28 September 1989

A Lockheed TR-1A (80-1082) of the 9th SRW landing at Beale AFB on 5 July 1988. The Bulldog on its tail appears to have quite a ferocious appetite for red stars

Above A TR-1A taxiing from the ramp to runway 15 at Beale AFB for a training sortie of 27 September 1989. The TR-1As and U-2Rs at Beale AFB are shared by the 5th and the 99th Strategic Reconnaissance Squadrons. Others are assigned to the 17th Reconnaissance Wing at RAF Alconbury, Huntingdon, and to Det 2 of the 9th SRW at Osan AB, Korea

Overleaf Assigned to the 193rd Special Operations Squadron, 193rd Special Operations Group, of the Pennsylvania Air National Guard, EC-130E(RR) psychological warfare aircraft have seen service over many parts of the world. This aircraft (63-7773) was photographed at Yokota AB, Japan, on 21 March 1989 *(Masanori Ogawa)*

Left A *Compass Call* EC-130H communications jamming aircraft of the 41st Electronic Combat Squadron, Tactical Air Command, doing touch-and-go landings at McClellan AFB in July 1986 *(Carl E Porter)*

Overleaf One of the early 'electronic wizards', only 35 RB-47Hs were built. The first of these electronic reconnaissance and countermeasures aircraft was delivered to the 55th SRW at Forbes AFB, Kansas, in August 1955. The last (53-4296) was photographed at Offutt AFB, Nebraska, on 29 December 1967 as it was about to depart on its ferry flight to the Military Aircraft Storage & Disposition Center at Davis-Monthan AFB, Arizona

Above This KC-135A (59-1465) was modified as a SIGINT (Signal Intelligence) platform as part of the *Rivet Stand* programme. Initially assigned to the 385th Strategic Aerospace Wing, it was operated by the 55th SRW when photographed at McClellan AFB on 2 September 1966. It crashed on 19 July 1967

Above RC-135S *Cobra Ball I* of the 6th SRW during a deployment from Eielson AFB in 1988. Along with another RC-135S (61-2662), this aircraft is used to track Soviet ballistic missiles and re-entry vehicles prior to impact on the Kamchatka Peninsula. Built as a C-135B, aircraft 61-2663 was coverted by LTV's E-Systems division into an RC-135S TELINT (Telemetry Intelligence) platform, the modification taking place in 1969 under the *Big Safari* programme *(Robert S Hopkins III)*

Above Photographed at Mather AFB on 18 November 1988, this aircraft was one of three RC-135Cs converted in 1971 by General Dynamics to RC-135U specs for the *Combat Sent* and *Combat Pink* programmes. Used extensively during the latter years of the Vietnam conflict, two of the three airframes converted still serve with the 55th SRW

Right Almost as rare as the aircraft itself, a *Combat Sent* patch is shown off by a 55th SRW crewman assigned to the highly modified RC-135U

The sole RC-135T (55-3121) crashed on 25 February 1985, just over seven months after it had been photographed during air refuelling over Alaska. This aircraft had been delivered by Boeing as a KC-135A and was successfully modified as a JKC-135A testbed for use by the Aeronautical Systems Division, a *Rivet Stand* SIGINT platform for assignment to the 55th SRW (first retaining the KC-135A designation but then being redesignated KC-135T), and as the thimble-nosed RC-135T *Cobra Jaws* reconnaissance platform. Retaining the RC-135T designation, 55-3121 was then used as a trainer for RC-135 pilots and navigators *(Carl E Porter)*

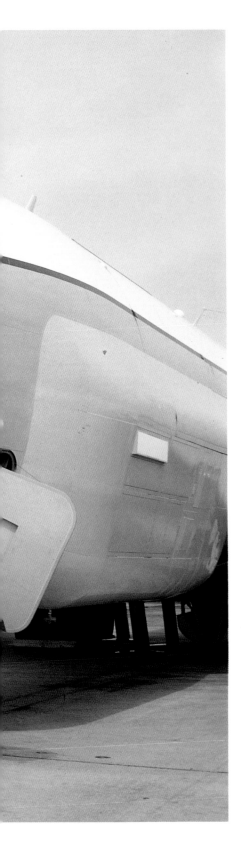

Left Some distance from home, this RC-135V (64-14843) was seen on the deck at Castle AFB, California, on 29 April 1989. The youngest of the eight-strong 55th SRW fleet, the aircraft is home based at Offutt in Nebraska

Below A *Rivet Joint* RC-135W (62-4131) of the 55th SRW at Beale AFB, California, on 5 June 1987. Notwithstanding what has been written in the past, the 'cheek' fairings on both sides for the forward fuselage of RC-135Cs, Us and Vs *never* contained a side-looking airborne radar (SLAR)! These fairings were provided to house a variety of sensors other than SLAR

Right A Grumman RV-1D of the 224th Military Intelligence Battalion, US Army, taking off from NAS Key West, Florida, on 8 October 1987. On that occasion two RV-1Ds took off from one runway, whilst a C-Span III configured U-2R was taking off from another runway. Coincidence, or joint intelligence gathering operations around Cuba or Central America?

Above Built and delivered as a U-21A Ute utility transport, 66-18003 was subsequently brought up to EU-21A standard for use by the Army Security Agency. It was photographed on 19 May 1969 at NAS Moffett Field, California, where it was operated by the US Army Air Mobility Research and Development Laboratory (AMRDL)

Right Although its name and acronym have been changed from US Army Air Mobility Research and Development Laboratory (ARMDL) to US Army Research and Technology Laboratories (AARTA), the Army unit based at NAS Moffett Field, California, remains most discrete. It was still AMRDL when this RU-21E was photographed on 18 May 1974

Above A US Army Sikorsky EH-60C (85-24473) at Mojave Airport, California, on 19 August 1987. The *Quick Fix IIB* communications jamming equipment was installed by Tracor Aerospace in its facilities at this airport in the Mojave Desert

The Lockheed EC-121M (WV-2Q before September 1962) gained notoriety on 14 April 1969 when an aircraft of VQ-1 was shot down in the Sea of Japan by North Korean fighters as it collected ELINT from an orbit over international waters. This EC-121M was photographed at the Military Aircraft Storage & Disposition Center, Davis-Monthan AFB, on 14 March 1976 after it had been withdrawn from use by VQ-1

Above and right The EC-121R version of the Lockheed Super Constellation was an airborne relay platform used during the Vietnam conflict. Flown by the 553rd Reconnaissance Wing, the aircraft sent information to the Dutch Mill Infiltration Surveillance Center at Nakhon Phanon RTAFB, this data having first been collected by seismic and acoustical sensors seeded along the Ho Chi Minh Trail and relayed to Pave Eagle QU-22B drones (modified Beech Bonanza light aircraft). Both aircraft were photographed at the Sacramento Air Logistics Center, the depot responsible for their support. The EC-121R (67-21477, ex-BuNo 141320) was seen on 25 October 1969 and the QU-22B (70-1536) on 22 May 1971

BuNo 150497, the first P-3A modified as an EP-3E ELINT/COMINT platform
by Hayes, at NAS Jacksonville, Florida, in July 1974 when it was accepted by
the USN *(Robert E Kling)*

An EA-3B of VQ-1 at Da Nang AB in December 1968. During the South-east Asian War this version of the Douglas Skywarrior collected valuable data on the North Vietnamese radar and communications network *(Ken Buchanan)*

Above BuNo 142673, an EA-3B fitted with an unidentified sensor in place of its tail turret, was photographed in April 1969

Right Thirty years after A3D-2Qs were first delivered to the Navy, fatigue problems finally forced the restriction of EA-3Bs (as A3D-2Qs had been redesignated in September 1962) from carrier operations. BuNo 142671 has just trapped aboard the USS *Constellation* (CV-64) during operations in the Indian Ocean on 3 March 1985, two and a half years before EA-3Bs were restricted to operations from land bases

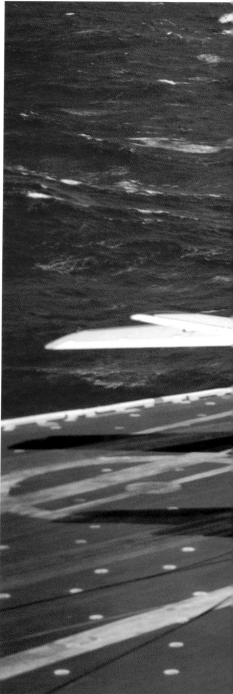

Command and Control

Right The US Navy pioneered the airborne early warning concept when it initiated *Project Cadillac* during World War 2. This programme saw a Grumman Avenger torpedo bomber modified into the prototype for an airborne early warning aircraft in the spring of 1944. Its twin-engined Grumman Tracer, the world's first aircraft designed specifically for the AEW role, entered·service in 1960. This aircraft from VAW-111 Det 14, assigned to CVSG-53 for deployment aboard the USS *Ticonderoga* (CVS-14), was photographed at NAS Lemoore, California, on 10 May 1970

Below BuNo 147209 from VAW-111 Det 2 was photographed in March 1974, two months after this detachment had returned from the last deployment of the USS *Hancock* (CVA-19)

Below Photographed on a sunny afternoon on the Miramar ramp in August 1988, these two Hawkeyes belong to the west coast E-2 Replacement Air Group (RAG) squadron, VAW-110. Having fulfilled the RAG requirements since the early 1960s, VAW-110 flew Grumman's earlier AEW efforts like the E-1B Tracer and the Bravo version of the Hawkeye, before receiving E-2Cs in the late 1970s *(Tony Holmes)*

Right Two E-2Cs from VAW-110 during carrier qualifications aboard the USS *Kitty Hawk* (CV-63) in March 1985

Above Home to six frontline AEW units and one reserve squadron, Miramar virtually overflows with Hawkeyes at times. Demonstrating standard E-2 taxiing procedures whilst ashore, a recently returned VAW-117 'Nighthawks' Hawkeye cruises down the ramp to its allotted spot on only one engine. Photographed soon after returning to Miramar following a lengthy and rather eventful WestPac cruise on board USS *Enterprise* (CVN-65), the 'Nighthawks' had featured prominently during *'Starship's'* war-at-sea in the Persian Gulf against the Iranian Navy. During this brief, but bloody skirmish in April 1988, VAW-117 had directed more than 80 fighter and 160 strike sorties for Air Wing 11 *(Tony Holmes)*

Left A Grumman E-2C (BuNo 158640) from the 'Hormel Hawgs' of VAW-114 flying over the desert east of NAS Fallon on 20 June 1989

Left A squadron also familiar with the Persian Gulf is VAW-113 'Black Eagles'. Attached to CVW-14 for a good few years, the 'Black Eagles' have spent many long hours over the past decade droning around in the clear blue skies above the Gulf. Sandwiched between two fellow 'Black Eagles' near *Constellation's* island, the squadron, along with the rest of CVW-14, have recently packed up their ready rooms and moved carriers to the newly refurbished USS *Independence* (CV-62), a move which has seen the *'Indy'* embark a full air wing for the first time in nearly five years *(Tony Holmes)*

Below Electronic warfare goes anti-drug; USCG 3501 (ex-BuNo 160968), one of two Grumman E-2Cs operated by the US Coast Guard over the Gulf of Mexico and the Caribbean from the Grumman facility at St Augustine, Florida, seen here at NAS Jacksonville in October 1987 *(Robert E Kling)*

Top Electronic support for the war against drug traffickers is provided by a variety of aircraft operated by several US government agencies. Notably, the US Customs Service is operating four modified Lockheed P-3As (including ex-BuNo 150514 photographed in April 1985 at NAS New Orleans, Louisiana) fitted with Hughes APG-63 radar to detect low flying aircraft *(Robert E Kling)*

Above BuNo 163918, one of the Boeing E-6As ordered by the US Navy as a replacement for its EC-130Gs and EC-130Qs,

Right Shall we use your frisbee or mine? A pair of Sentries from the 552nd Airborne Warning and Control Wing (AW & CW) (E-3A 77-0351 in the foreground and E-3C 83-0008 in the background) preparing to depart from Tinker AFB on 1 May 1989

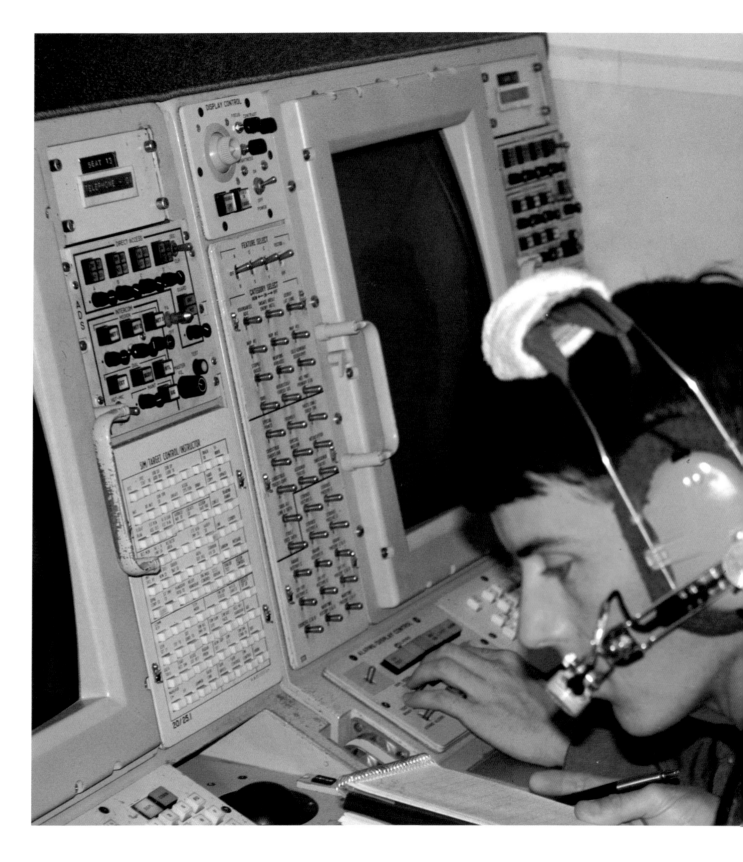

Previous pages Boeing E-3C (80-0139) of the 965th AW & CS, 552nd AW & CW, lifting off from runway 17 at Tinker AFB. The Rockwell B-1B in the background is parked on the ramp of the Oklahoma City Air Force Logistics Center, the AFLC facility responsible for B-1B support and overhaul

Left Two 2Lt trainees in one of the two mission simulators of the 552nd AW & CW. One of the simulators is used to train mission crews for standard configured (Core) Sentries and the other to train crews for standard and upgraded (Block 25) aircraft. Following academic training with the 552nd Tactical Training Squadron, mission crews receive airborne training with the 966th Airborne Warning and Control Training Squadron, both units being based at Tinker AFB as part of the 552nd AW & CW

Below Boeing E-3A (77-0351) of the 552nd AW & CW at Tinker AFB, Oklahoma, on 1 May 1989. The black fin and intake covers denote that this aircraft belongs to the 963rd AW & C Squadron

Above Wingtip taxiing light ablaze, a recently returned E-3A Sentry is carefully marshalled back to the squadron ramp at Tinker

Left Most Air Force EC-135s are 'camera shy' on the ground. This EC-135J belongs to the 7th Airborne Command and Control Squadron (ACCS), a PACAF unit assigned to the 15th Air Base Wing at Hickam AFB, Hawaii. The 7th ACCS keeps an EC-135 detachment at March AFB, California, where 62-3584 is seen landing in January 1984

Left Green Flag: a Lockheed EC-130E Airborne Battlefield Command and Control Center of the 7th ACCS lands at Nellis AFB in July 1987

Above BuNo 156171, the second EC-130Q TACAMO airborne communications relay aircraft, landing at McClellan AFB on 17 January 1989. On the ground, EC-130Qs are usually kept in out-of-the-way apron areas and are guarded by armed personnel, photography being seldom permitted

Electronic Warfare

Besides the 390th Electronic Combat Squadron at Mountain Home AFB, Idaho, the 42nd ECS, 20th TFW, at RAF Upper Heyford, is the only other operational unit to be equipped with EF-111As. It received its first 'Spark Varks' in February 1984 and achieved notoriety in April 1986 when it provided electronic support during *Operation Eldorado Canyon* the US retaliatory raid against Libya (*Jean-Michel Guhl*)

Below With its sturdy landing gear firmly locked down, and its massive variable geometry wings swept fully forward, EF-111A 66-0039 of the 42nd ECS, 66th ECW, recovers at McClellan on 12 January 1989

Right Perhaps the best looking 'electronic wizard' of them all, the EF-111A Raven has the 'beam-bite' to match its handsome lines. Refuelling receptacle agape, a 'Spark Vark' is eased towards the flying boom of a KC-135R by its experienced 42nd ECS pilot. The small horns mounted on either side of the aircraft's spine contain receiver antennae which form part of the EF-111's self-defence system. Directly slaved to the AN/ALR-62(V)-4 terminal threat warning system, which is in turn part of the formidable Sanders AN/ALQ-137(V)-4 ECM self-protection suite, the receivers cover emissions in the low, medium and high-band frequencies (*Air Portraits*)

Above In 1964, when air operations over North Vietnam began, the only jet-powered tactical electronic warfare aircraft in service with US naval forces was venerable Douglas EF-10B, modified from the 1950-vintage F3D-2 night fighter, and operated by two Marine Composite Reconnaissance Squadrons, VMCJ-1 and VMCJ-3. This aircraft from VMCJ-3 was photographed at MCAS E1 Toro in May 1965. The last Marine EF-10Bs were retired on 31 May 1970

Opposite above Modified from A-3B carrier-based heavy attack aircraft, the EKA-3B was a dual-role ECM support-tanker aircraft. The six stripes around the rear fuselage indicate that this was the sixth aircraft from VAQ-131. Assigned to CVW-1, this squadron was then getting ready for deployment to the Mediterranean Sea aboard the USS *John F Kennedy* (CV-67). That deployment lasted from 14 September 1970 to 1 March 1971

Opposite below Photographed at NAS Alameda, California, on 24 September 1971, this EKA-3B of VQ-130 Det 1 departed one week later aboard the USS *Constellation* (CV-64) for a nine-month combat deployment to the Gulf of Tonkin

Left   To replace its EF-10Bs, the Marine Corps obtained 27 Grumman
EA-6As (six modified from A-6A airframes and 21 new-build aircraft). These
two-seat aircraft entered service with VMCJ-2 at MCAS Cherry Point, North
Carolina, in December 1965, and later equipped VMCJ-1 at NAS Atsugi, Japan,
and VMCJ-3 at MCAS El Toro, California. This VMCJ-3 aircraft was
photographed at NAS Miramar on 16 March 1974

Above An ex-Marine EA-6A in the markings of VAQ-309, a Navy
reserve unit, taxiing at NAS Fallon, Nevada, on 3 May 1980

Left Quietly sitting on the reserve ramp at beautiful NAS Whidbey Island, Washington State, this weary 'Electric Intruder' awaits its two-man crew. The 'Axe Men' of VAQ-309 have been performing the ECM role for Reserve Air Wing 30 since the late 1970s when they formed up on surplus VMAQ-2 EA-6As, the latter unit trading up to Prowlers. Regularly overhauled at the Naval Aircraft Rework Facility (NARF) at NAS North Island, California, the EA-6As have given the Navy and Marine Corps over 25 years of solid ECM service *(Tony Holmes)*

Below Birdcage open and engine covers agape, this particular airframe was one of 15 new-build EA-6As built by Grumman in the mid-1960s. In its subtle greys, the ferocious 'Sea Hawk' motif emblazoned on the antenna fairing is almost lost from sight. If you are an American football fan you will have probably recognized that the 'bird' is in fact a low-viz version of the blue, white and green emblem which dominates the helmets of Seattle's NFL team, the Sea Hawks. The unique EA-6As no longer grace the blue skies above Whidbey Island as VAQ-309 became the first reserve unit to receive the Prowler in mid-1989, this transition completing the 'horizontal integration' (!) of CVWR-30 with frontline aircraft *(Tony Holmes)*

Previous pages As Prowlers were not included in CVW-13 for deployment aboard the USS *Coral Sea* (CV-43), the 'Black Ravens' of VAQ-135 quickly sent a detachment to the Mediterranean Sea to serve aboard the *'Coral Maru'* during *Operation Eldorado Canyon* against Libya in April 1986. BuNo 161349 was photographed at NAS Whidbey Island, after returning home following this short but eventful deployment *(Rick Morgan)*

Right Prowler on the prowl; an EA-6B ICAP 1 from the 'Cougars' of VAQ-139 during RefTra (Refresher Training) aboard the USS *Constellation* (CV-64) in February 1986 *(Rick Morgan)*

Left Captured on a sun drenched Whidbey ramp on a crisp July morning, this blotchy machine belongs to VAQ-137 'Rooks', the squadron having just returned from a det to NAS Fallon with the rest of CVW-1. Whilst at the 'biggest little air station in the world', the 'Rooks' took full advantage of the excellent EW range set up for visiting VAQ squadrons. Fully equipped with TACTS interface that allows ground controllers to simulate real world threats from Soviet SAMs and *Gun Dish* radar, the 'Echo Whiskey' range teaches both new and experienced crews the latest techniques of ECM warfare *(Tony Holmes)*

Above VAQ-137 were the seventh Prowler squadron activated by the Navy in December 1973, their Aztec-influenced Rook becoming a familiar trademark of the unit. While attached to USS *John F Kennedy* (CV-67) in 1983, the 'Rooks' flew ECM sorties against Syrian radar during the ill-fated Alpha strike on terrorist positions in the Lebanon, their exact role in the mission still remaining classified. The prominent 'sawtooth' at the base of the refuelling probe houses an AN/ALQ-125 radar receiver *(Tony Holmes)*

Overleaf BuNo 158304, an EA-6B ICAP 2 of VAQ-129, the Prowler training squadron based at NAS Whidbey Island *(Rick Morgan)*

Left An EA-6B from the 'Garudas' of VAQ-134 returning from a training sortie at NAS Fallon on 21 June 1989 before a deployment aboard the *USS Carl Vinson* (CVN-70)

Above Separated by almost a decade, these two photos perfectly illustrate the drastic colour change which has enveloped Navy and Marine Corps squadrons throughout the fleet. Having flown the two-seat EA-6A for many years, VMAQ-2 eventually adorned the far more capable EA-6B with its distinctive 'Black Bunny' emblem in September 1977. 'Triple-Nuts' Prowler 160432 was photographed heading up a line of 'Bunnies' at NAS North Island during a full squadron stopover in San Diego in September 1978. Looking decidedly 'grey' by comparison, 'Bunny 02' was one of three EA-6Bs that trekked all the way from MCAS Cherry Point in North Carolina to Royal Australian Air Force Base Pearce in Western Australia for exercise Valiant Usher '87. The radar jamming power of this aircraft, equipped with five ALQ-99 pods, would give any 'enemy' ground controller a considerable headache! *(Second photo by Tony Holmes)*

Below Looking a little worse for wear, an EB-66E, 54-0446 of the 19th Tactical Electronic Warfare Squadron (TEWS) quietly reposes between sorties at McClellan AFB in April 1968. Basically a rebuild of the RB-66B, 145 Echo model EB-66s were produced by Douglas. Jam packed with an upgraded EW suite, the EBs performed tirelessly over Vietnam despite their age and rather troublesome twin Allison J71-A-13 turbojets

Right The 4417th Combat Crew Training Squadron was activated in the 363rd Tactical Reconnaissance Wing at Shaw AFB on 1 July 1966 to train EB-66 crews for service with TAC, PACAF, and USAFE. It was redesignated 39th Tactical Reconnaissance Training Squadron in February 1967, and 39th Tactical Electronic Warfare Training Squadron (TEWTS) in October 1969. This EB-66E of the 39th TEWTS was photographed at Davis-Monthan AFB on 19 March 1974, four days after the squadron became the last EB/RB-66 unit to be inactivated

Electronic Aggressors

Douglas ERA-3B (BuNo 144846) from VAQ-34, one of the latest Tactical Electronic Warfare Squadrons commissioned in the US Navy, flying off the coast of Southern California on 13 January 1986 *(Rick Morgan)*

Right In 1970 VAQ-33 became the first flying unit of the Fleet Electronic Warfare Support Group (FEWSG). Since then the 'Firebirds' have made considerable use of specially configured A-3Bs and ERA-3Bs, including BuNo 144832 seen landing at NAS Key West, Florida, on 8 October 1987

Below Although more of a museum piece than a current frontline type, the venerable ERA-3 continues to put in valuable time helping to train sailors and aircrew in the art of ECM warfare. This well-kept machine was photographed in VAQ-33 colours on 8 October 1987

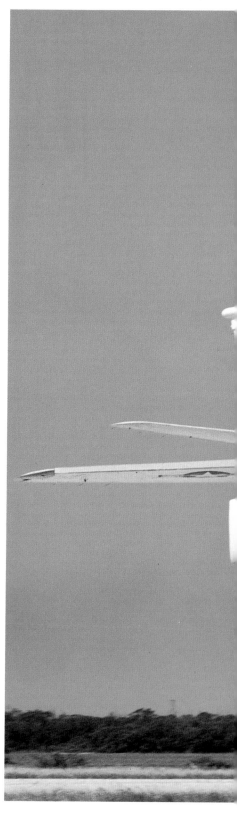

Left Along with Skywarriors, VAQ-33 has long operated two-seat Skyhawks. BuNo 152869, which was photographed at NAS Miramar, California, on 11 October 1975, was one of the few to bear the EA-4F designation

Above NAS Key West, 9 October 1987. Still wearing its standard TA-4J designation, this Skyhawk of VAQ-33 (BuNo 158136) has been configured as an electronic aggressor with an AN/AST-4 jammer beneath its port wing

Left and top Because of a Navy-wide shortage of TA-4Js, VAQ-34 received EA-7Ls to supplement its ERA-3Bs. BuNo 156741 and its crew, Lt(jg) Nancy Dykhoff and Lt Lori Melling, were photographed whilst taking part in an airshow at Beale AFB, California, on 10 August 1988

Above The VAQ-34 crews were known as the 'Electric Horsemen.' In the case of Lisa 'Ratwoman' Nowak, this appears to be somewhat of a misnomer

Left One of the more obscure types operated by VAQ-33 is the EA-6A 'Electric Intruder,' this particular machine being spotted on det to NAS Jacksonville. According to its BuNo, this airframe was the second production A-6 built by Grumman way back in 1960! When it first left the factory, the aircraft still had the original unsloped vertical tail associated with the very early pre-production Intruders

Above The largest aircraft operated by VAQ-33 has been the NC-121/EC-121. BuNo 141292 was designated NC-121K and coded GD11 when photographed at NAS Miramar on 11 October 1975. However, when photographed a year later at North Island the aircraft had been modified to EC-121P configuaration and coded GD12

Overleaf The replacement aircraft for the NC/EC-121 is the EP-3A. BuNo 150592 was photographed at NAS Key West, VAQ-33's home, on 8 October 1987

To supplement aircraft operated by VAQ-33 and VAQ-34, the Fleet Electronic
Warfare Support Group first acquired two ex-Air Force B-47Es. These aircraft
were modified and operated for FEWSG by McDonnell Douglas. Photographed
at Davis-Monthan AFB on 14 March 1976, this Douglas-built NB-47E bears its
Air Force radio call number on the fin, the word NAVY on its forward fuselage,
and the MASDC inventory number 1B007 on its nose wheel door

The most recent addition to the FEWSG fleet is the sole EC-24A, BuNo 163050. Built as a DC-8-54AF (s/n 45881, N8048U), this aircraft had flown over 42,000 hours before being sold by United Air Lines in November 1984. It was modified for FEWSG by Electrospace Systems Inc of Richardson, Texas, and delivered to the Navy in August 1987. Principal mission equipment includes radar and communication jamming systems, chaff dispensers, ESM receivers, direction finding systems, and HF/UHF/VHF transceivers. The mission crew consists of a pilot, co-pilot, flight engineer, and seven system operators (one of which is the mission commander) *(Mick Roth)*

Left Between 1959, when the 4677th and 4713th Defence Systems Evaluation Squadrons (DSES) were activated, and 1982, when the 134th DSES, Vermont ANG, was re-equipped with F-4Ds, various models of the Martin B-57 twin-jet were used by both active and Guard units as electronic aggressors. This EB-57B of the 134th DSES is on final approach after playing the role of an enemy aircraft during 'William Tell' '78 at Tyndall AFB, Florida

Above Equally long lasting as an electronic aggressor was the Lockheed T-33A. Carrying a jammer pod beneath the starboard wing and a chaff pod beneath the port wing, this aircraft of the 84th Fighter Interceptor Squadron at Castle AFB, California, taxies out for a training sortie on 7 October 1976 during which it served as an intercept target for the unit's F-106As. Since the Air Force and the Air Guard phased out their T-33As in 1988, Flight International has been under contract to provide Learjet 25s and 35s and Mitsubishi MU-2s fitted with electronic warfare equipment to serve as aggressors

Electronic RDT&E

Looking absolutely resplendent in its Air Force Systems Command white over light grey scheme, an early production KC-135A of the 4950th Test Wing taxies in to McClellan AFB on 25 February 1968. Currently still flying with the Test Wing out of Wright-Patterson AFB, the aircraft has been modified to NKC-135A specs since this fine portrait was taken. One of eight NKCs in the 4950th fleet, the aircraft performs many diverse roles including ECM/ECCM, laser, ionosphere, icing, comsat, missile vulnerability, boom and weightless research, amongst other things!

Above The Aeronautical Systems Division, Air Force Systems Command, at Wright-Patterson AFB, Ohio, has used C-135s in many interesting configurations. This NKC-135A (55-3131), photographed at McClellan AFB on 17 September 1973, has a row of seven rectangular windows on the upper starboard fuselage side, and a plexiglass dome on its rear fuselage

Right Eight C-135As (including 60-0375 photographed at McClellan AFB on 12 March 1974) were modified as EC-135Ns by Douglas as part of the Advanced Range Instrumented Aircraft (ARIA) project to provide telemetry for the Apollo space programme

Right The steerable dish antenna mounted within the bulbous radome of the EC-135N was the largest ever carried by an aircraft, this close-up view taken at McClellan clearly showing the unique modification. Replaced in the ARIA role by a pair of ex-civilian Boeing 707s (designated EC-18As in USAF service), four of the EC-135Ns have been re-engined with Pratt & Whitney TF33s and now serve as trials aircraft, designated EC-135Es.

Below One of the four EC-135Ns (60-0374, 61-0326, 61-0329 and 61-033) converted to EC-135E specs. Aircraft 61-0326 was photographed at Edwards AFB on 13 August 1986

Left With the Navy, the counterparts of the EC/NKC-135s of the Air Force Systems Command are Lockheed P-3 Orion patrol aircraft modified for various test purposes. This EP-3A of VX-1, on the transient aircraft ramp at NAS Fallon on 10 May 1976, had a truncated nose radome, a non-standard ventral radome, and wingtip pods

Above A close-up of the forward fuselage of the EP-3A shows how heavily the formerly curved radome has been flattened, and just how large the fairing covering the E-systems ALD-8 radio direction finder is. An aircraft with a long and distinguished past, this particular airframe served as the prototype EP-3A for the Naval Air Test Center (NATC) in the late 1960s. Following its time with the NATC, the aircraft then went to the Naval Weapons Laboratory (NWL), before entering squadron service with Air Test & Evaluation Squadron One (VX-1)

Above The Naval Air Development Center at Warminster, Pennsylvania, has recently been conducting laser research with a pair of modified UP-3As. BuNo 152150, seen at NAS Jacksonville on 18 December 1989, has a laser-emitting device above the fuselage, whereas the all-grey BuNo 148889 appears to be used to measure laser beam strength and diffusion

Previous page Landing at McClellan AFB on 8 July 1988, this EP-3A (BuNo 150409) of the Pacific Missile Test Center (PMTC) shows the distinctive extension of its vertical fin which houses a Raytheon Rotman-lense phase array antenna. The modification of this aircraft into an extended area test system (EATS) airborne instrumentation station was realized by Hayes International of Birmingham, Alabama

Lockheed EP-3E (BuNo 150520) of the PMTC, at NAS New Orleans, in September 1984

Left This more mundane ES-2D (BuNo 147532), photographed at NAS Point Mugu on 5 November 1977, was fitted with loud speakers in underwing nacelles to warn off vessels that had strayed into the restricted Pacific Missile Test Range off the coast of California

Above Fitted with a steerable phase-array antenna in a fairing on the starboard side of the fuselage, two civil-registered de Havilland Canada E-9As are used as airborne surveillance platforms in support of missile and drone testing out of Tyndall AFB, Florida

The most photographed NRA-3B operated by the PMTC at NAS Point Mugu
was BuNo 144825. It had been fitted with a distinctive bulbous nose by
Grumman in 1960 to test the pulse doppler radar and missile control system for
the AAM-N-10 Eagle long-range air-to-air missile then being developed by a
Bendix/Grumman team. 'Snoopy', as the aircraft was affectionately known at
Point Mugu, has recently been fitted with a 'new' nose from a stricken
Skywarrior the work being performed by Chrysler Technology Airborne
Systems of Waco, Texas

A Lockheed EC-121K at NAS North Island, California, on 26 August 1967. The aircraft had been specially modified for use at the Pacific Missile Range, NAS Point Mugu, California, and had been fitted with pairs of additional radomes above the forward fuselage and beneath the rear fuselage. BuNo 137890 was placed in storage at the Military Aircraft Storage & Disposition Center, Davis-Monthan AFB, on 7 May 1979

The sign says it all . . .